Spiritual Healing Guide: How to Heal Yourself and Others Using Spiritual Methods

Chakra, Reiki and Theta Healing Guides for Spiritual Healing

Stacy Milescu

I want to dedicate this book to everyone who craves more knowledge about the spiritual world. I hope this book will edify and enlighten you.

Copyright © 2014 by Speedy Publishing LLC

All rights reserved. No part of this publication may be reproduced, distributed or transmitted in any form or by any means, including photocopying, recording, or other electronic or mechanical methods, without the prior written permission of the publisher, except in the case of brief quotations embodied in critical reviews and certain other noncommercial uses permitted by copyright law. For permission requests, write to the publisher, addressed "Attention: Permissions Coordinator," at the address below.

Speedy Publishing LLC (c) 2014
40 E. Main St., #1156
Newark, DE 19711
www.speedypublishing.co

Ordering Information:
Quantity sales; Special discounts are available on quantity purchases by corporations, associations, and others. For details, contact the "Special Sales Department" at the address above.

-- 1st edition

Manufactured in the United States of America

TABLE OF CONTENTS

PUBLISHER'S NOTES i

CHAPTER 1: WHAT IS SPIRITUAL HEALING? 1

CHAPTER 2: THETA HEALING 9

CHAPTER 3: THE CHAKRAS 13

CHAPTER 4: REIKI AND SPIRITUAL HEALING 21

MEET THE AUTHOR 27

MORE BOOKS BY STACY MILESCU 28

Publisher's Notes

Disclaimer

This publication is intended to provide helpful and informative material. It is not intended to diagnose, treat, cure, or prevent any health problem or condition, nor is intended to replace the advice of a physician. No action should be taken solely on the contents of this book. Always consult your physician or qualified health-care professional on any matters regarding your health and before adopting any suggestions in this book or drawing inferences from it.

The author and publisher specifically disclaim all responsibility for any liability, loss or risk, personal or otherwise, which is incurred as a consequence, directly or indirectly, from the use or application of any contents of this book.

Any and all product names referenced within this book are the trademarks of their respective owners. None of these owners have sponsored, authorized, endorsed, or approved this book.

Always read all information provided by the manufacturers' product labels before using their products. The author and publisher are not responsible for claims made by manufacturers.

Print Edition 2014

Chapter 1: What Is Spiritual Healing?

Spirituality refers to the recognition and acceptance of a God that is outside of our own aptitude and with whom we can establish a relationship. God is able to provide an incidence of guidance, along with peace of mind, security, joy, and inspiration that can carry us beyond what can happen in times of doubt.

Any time energy is sent to an individual who needs it, it is known as spiritual healing. This form of treatment works on the spirit, mind and body which can be viewed as a whole. It needs to be in balance for our health. Spiritual healing can assist with emotional and mental problems as well as any physical problems.

The transmission of healing energy from a spiritual source to an individual who needs it is known as spiritual healing. The channel is typically an individual known as a healer. The energy to provide healing is typically transferred to the patient through the hands of the healer. Bear in mind that the healer does not provide the healing, but he or she is merely a vessel that transmits it. Note that a healer is not necessary to receive the benefits of spiritual healing.

Prayer is always an option.

When the word *spiritual* is used, it refers to energy's divine nature, which is said to come from one invisible, external, intelligent source. The energy of healing from this source can be accessed by all.

Healers view the spirit, mind and body as one co-dependent unit; all three have to work in synchronization to remain healthy. If there are any challenges, whether it is depression or a broken limb, the power of healing can bring everything back into balance. On a spiritual level, it's believed that sickness begins deep in the spirit or in the mind, and that is where the healing often begins.

The New Age and the Start of a New Epoch

The term New Age generally refers to multiple elements, from knowledge of the connections of the body and mind to programs for self-improvement, which can grow exponentially.

In 1996, Time magazine reported that approximately 44 million Americans identified with spiritual healing. It is also thought that approximately $1.5 billion is spent on books centered on religion and spirituality each year. Approximately 42% of people in the United States have used alternative health care.

James Redfield, author of "The Celestial Prophecy," says that there is a hunger to be connected with a divine power, as much for the experience as for the philosophy of it, and a harmony of awareness is a chance for growth.

Religion vs. Spirituality

Religion is different from spirituality. Various religions in the world have put forward numerous belief systems and doctrines of belief about the personality of a God and the corresponding relationship humans have with God. When it comes to spirituality, it speaks to the typical experience regarding these numerous points of view.

Everyone is free to see God as they wish, whether in the majestic beauty of the mountains or the oceans, or just as an abstract being. Even an atheist or an agnostic may receive some sort of stimulation from watching the sun-set, or going for a walk through the woods. A baby's smile can bring that same sense of joy.

Harvard University's Dr. Herbert Benson, author of The Relaxation Response, carried out a number of experiments to establish the worth of mantra or prayer. Dr. Benson was of the belief that the mantra had no magical qualities to it. He had participants meditate using a phrase or word that they were comfortable with.

He also did case studies on Jews and Christians who prayed on a regular basis. Protestants used the first line of the 23rd Psalm, *The Lord Is my Shepherd*, or the first line of the Lord's Prayer, Jews were asked to use *Echad* or *Shalom* and the Catholics were asked to use the Jesus prayer, or to repeat a phrase like, "Hail Mary, full of grace."

Each of the phrases worked to trigger relaxation and beneficial physiological changes. In addition, Benson also discovered that the individuals who made use of a phrase or word not linked to any spiritual belief failed to stick to the program. Those who used religious phrases or words stayed with the practice.

Scientists have shown that these mantras or prayers are indeed effective. A person using them needs to believe in their power in order for them to work. (This is referred to as intrinsic belief by scientists.)

Religion is typified by a quest or devotion for a different life and a deep commitment to spirituality. As such, the religious aspect of spirituality is extremely useful and may be necessary before the total advantages of spiritual healing can be achieved.

Healing can be acquired by growing ones spiritual life. Personal dedication is the most essential aspect of the entire process. Spiritual growth and awareness can generate a total transformation. It can assist with the development of basic faith and a trust that is unwavering - the core of intrinsic belief.

Many believe that having a relationship with God gives them the faith, hope, courage and moral support they need to go through with their program of personal healing. It gives them a feeling that they are not alone in the cosmos, and that there exists a power that provides support and guidance that can be accessed in times of discouragement and confusion.

Benefits of Developing Spirituality

Edmund Bourne, the author of *The Anxiety and Phobia Workbook*, outlined a number of advantages to spirituality as it pertains to dealing with the healing of emotional challenges.

Safety and Security

By establishing a connection with God, one gains a feeling of security through the belief that he or she is not the only one in the cosmos, especially during moments of loss or separation. With the belief that there is a power to look to during a challenge, the feeling of safety increases.

Serenity

Serenity or peace of mind comes from feeling a profound, long-lasting feeling of safety and security. The more trust and reliance in God, the easier it is to exist without worry or fear of the challenges that come in life.

Bear in mind that the will and the self are not surrendered to this source of power; instead, spiritual seekers learn that it is okay to release burdens onto God when they are stuck in a challenging situation and have no option out.

Understanding how to let go when a problem can't be solved immediately can help to lessen the anxiety in life. Serenity can fill the void that the lack of anxiety leaves.

Self-Assurance

When building a relationship with God, many begin to realize that because they were created by God, they are entitled to respect, and are lovable and good.

Being aware of this will improve the way *you* view yourself and how you think about yourself (ego). You are valuable and naturally good, if you are a part of the cosmos as everything else is.

The Ability to Receive and Give Love Unconditionally

The most basic feature of God is that God provides the experience of love that is unconditional. It is a type of love that is different from ordinary friendship or romantic love. It embodies the unlimited awareness and caring for the welfare of another person without any requirements, without judging them.

As you get closer to God, you start to experience higher levels of this type of love in your life. Your heart is more attuned to the concerns and needs of others. You feel much freer. There is no need for comparisons or judgments. This type of love manifests both in your increased ability to share love with others and to get more in return. There is much more joy and less fear in your life, and you help motivate others to explore their own ability to love. It can be seen in having all that you require to do as well as what you need to do.

Guidance

Establishing a relationship with God supplies the help needed to solve problems and make decisions. God has a universal wisdom that surpasses what we can achieve with our own knowledge. In the conventional religions, this is known as divine intelligence.

When you connect with God, you are able to call upon this higher level of intellect to help solve a myriad of problems.

The answer that you get may be more than you expected. God is literally guiding you through. He is always there to help those who wait patiently for Him to provide guidance and insight.

Building a Relationship with God

Always be open, patient and quiet before God.

Always have the faith that He will indicate wants and will help you to get them done.

Never make terms with God or tempt Him. As Gandhi said, "You have to be extremely humble to eradicate any evil that you have inside of you." God requires that you give of yourself completely as it is the only way to be completely free.

Be willing to take what God provides as He knows what is best for you. You must trust in His wisdom.

God is there to help, so ask Him for it. Never instruct.

Allow God to use His word to communicate with you. Read religious and spiritual books like the Bible and learn all that you can.

These practices can all help a great deal with your process toward personal healing.

CHAPTER 2: THETA HEALING

What exactly is Theta Healing?

Theta healing is not work on the body. Instead it is a type of primeval spiritual practice of healing through prayer. It is founded on the basis that all beings are linked and that beings are also connected to the primary source (God). Theta healing is not dangerous. It can help an individual in a number of ways on an unconscious and conscious level.

The healers that practice Theta have training in basic techniques of meditation, which allows them to make the connection to the Source by reducing their brain waves to the Theta level. After getting the permission of the client, they can offer a prayer for changes to occur and also see the change occur when the Source responds.

Bear in mind that Theta healers do not perform the healing alone. They work alongside the client to figure out what may need to be changed.

This may be adjusting a belief in the subconscious, healing a physical problem, or making use of one of other techniques and tools that are available with this type of healing. When an agreement is reached, the healer will authorize the healing to happen through prayer. The healer will then take his or her place as observer and witness the healing.

Applied Quantum Physics

Applied quantum physics is Theta Healing. The study of quantum physics studies energy matter at the deepest, most subtle levels. Until recent times, the thought of using prayer to heal seemed contrary to scientific precepts. Belief in the ways that prayer can heal was often thought to be superstitious in scientific circles; this attitude more often than not placed spiritual persons and scientists on opposite sides of the fence when it came to the true value of prayer.

Modern day discoveries in quantum physics, however, have indicated that there is a powerful force in consciousness.

As healers bring their brainwaves to the Theta level, the barriers of ego disappear, and in that level of consciousness they are better able to connect to the cosmic consciousness we've named God.

The theory of quantum non locality indicates that a linking connection can be present between two or more things, even if they are far apart. If a single object is agitated, the other will react and appear to feel it, no matter how far apart they are.

This non-locality indicates that conscious prayer can be used to promote change. From an ethical point of view, Theta Healing needs the will to be healed to be stated by those seeking the healing before the offered.

The theory about quantum entanglement indicates that the process of looking at a quantum particle will cause a change in its behavior (meaning that consciousness does have an effect on events in the substantial world). For instance, research in the field of microbiology indicates that human emotion can either loosen or constrict the way in which human DNA displays on a microscopic slide.

The DNA strands become looser or tighter based on the way the person *looking at it* is feeling while studying it. This is the same principle that Theta healers rely upon as they observe changes that occur.

How Theta Healing Came To Be

Theta healing was originally known as the Orion Technique. This technique is really a version of remote viewing. This form of prayer that heals was revived and reintroduced in 1995 to the post-modern world by Vianna Stibal, an author, artist, grandmother, healer, and medical intuitive. Carrying out the instructions that she received from God, she used particular methods. When doctors told her she had terminal cancer and advised her she only had weeks to live, she was miraculously healed. From then on she took it upon herself to share what she had learned with others.

A Typical Theta Healing Session

Practitioners of Theta will start by carrying out an energetic scan on the person seeking healing, helping them to decide through the use of intuition the areas that are dysfunctional or diseased. Then he or she will move on to the next step and ask the client particular questions to figure out exactly what the client wants to change. A kind of applied kinesiology (also known as muscle testing) will be used to confirm what the client senses.

As soon as the practitioner has entered the state of Theta, he or she will then make the link the Supreme Force to start the process of healing, whether the healing involves issues with social conditioning, patterns of thought, or general health.

Healings cannot be carried out unless verbal consent is given. The individual and healers work together as co-makers with God to bring more health, abundance and happiness to the client through adjustments in root beliefs.

The Only Healer is The Divine Source or God

These types of healings can cover a number of conditions, including troubling memories, thoughts, emotions and physical problems that might be causing distress or illness.

Theta Healing operates on four tiers:

Core Beliefs: learning and conditioning from the time of conception.

Genetic Beliefs: inherited DNA, further found in the DNA structure of an individual (that provides instructions to the DNA).

History Beliefs: principles like racial memories that come from the collective consciousness.

Soul Level: the essential, individual and impressionable part of the true nature that we possess which makes us beings who are linked to a Higher Source.

Theta Healing is dedicated to reaching lasting, proper and permanent outcomes.

CHAPTER 3: THE CHAKRAS

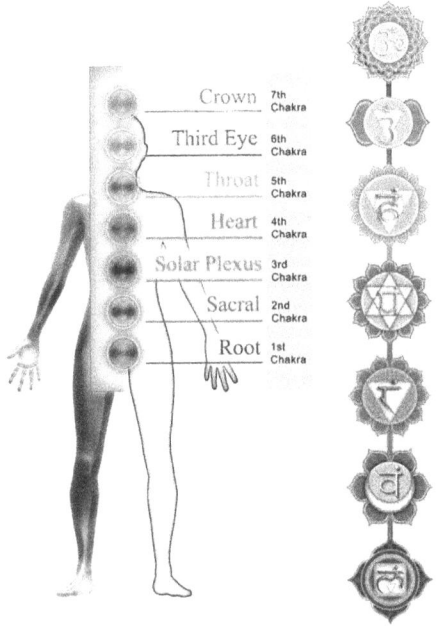

A Definition

Chakra is from the Sanskrit word meaning "wheel," but in a more precise translation is "spinning wheel." If you were able to see the chakras (as many persons who work with them can), you would be able to see each main chakra as a wheel of energy or a spinning vortex. This spinning starts from the front of the body and spins in toward the center on the kundalini (spiritual energy in a dormant form) of that chakra, then spins out from that point from the rear of the body.

Locations of the Chakras

The chakras begin at the base of the spine and then go up to the head on the kundalini that rests close to the spinal column. Kundalini resembles a staff and is referenced in the 23rd Psalm in the Bible. Typically all religions mention energy and spiritual power points in the body.

There are 7 main chakras and approximately 100 secondary smaller chakras. The smaller points are typically referred to as meridians and are utilized during the process of acupuncture to help atune the flow of Chi. The secondary points are affected by physicality and action, while the main chakra points are influenced by spirituality and emotions.

The main chakras have an influence on individual health. Issues with health are linked to any imbalance in a chakra either from a spiritual or emotional perspective. This then shows as a physical illness. Bear in mind that each chakra has a strong link to a specific part of the body, to spiritual and mental issues, and to particular emotions.

The main chakras have an influence on individual health. Issues with health are linked to any imbalance in a chakra either from a spiritual or emotional perspective. This then shows as a physical illness. Bear in mind that each chakra has a strong link to a specific part of the body, to spiritual and mental issues, and to particular emotions.

1st Chakra – Root

When finances are at a low and you find yourself stressing, you could end up seeing red. The color red is associated with the Root Chakra. The Root Chakra is located in close proximity to your tailbone and can affect the way we look at issues of survival, safety and security. The Root Chakra is also related to being grounded and connected with the Mother Earth.

2nd Chakra – Belly (Sacral)

When you think about the color orange, think about Sacral Chakra, which is all about our sexuality, pleasure and the sense of having plenty. Located in the lower abdomen, a couple inches below your navel, this area can improve on our creative desires as we work towards accepting change. Sacral Chakra is also important in our attempts to accept new things.

3rd Chakra – Solar Plexus

If you are lacking in self-confidence, or your self-esteem is lower than normal, you are probably having issues with your Solar Plexus Chakra. The upper abdomen in the stomach is home to this Chakra and its main color is yellow. The Solar Plexus Chakra is the center of personal power and where the developments of psychic abilities occur.

4th Chakra – Heart

The colors pink and green are affiliated with the heart Chakra. This chakra is the center for inner peace, joy, love, compassion and spirituality. You can find the heart Chakra above the heart, in the middle of your chest. This Chakra is very important for health reasons and for giving and receiving love, especially since it can affect the way we love others.

5th Chakra – Throat

People who have trouble communicating or hold back on telling others how they really feel, might be feeling a little blue. The Throat Chakra is associated with a light blue color. The Throat Chakra is located at the throat, hence the name, and is where anger is stored or let go of. This Chakra can affect our ability to keep secrets or speak our truth. This Chakra may be improved through some choice melodies and even a little chanting.

6th Chakra – Third Eye (Brow)

When things are a little fuzzy, or we simply have trouble seeing the whole picture, we could have issues with the third eye Chakra. Located on our foreheads, right in the middle of our natural eyes, this Indigo colored Chakra is all about our imagination, or lack thereof. The importance of the third eye Chakra should not be taken lightly, especially since it can affect our ability to make important decisions.

7th Chakra – Crown

The Crown Chakra is located at the top of the human head and associated with the color violet. This Chakra controls both inner and outer beauty and is the foundation of our spiritual body. This Chakra influences our spiritual beliefs, inspiration and idealism. Pure bliss can be felt when this Chakra is open and functioning properly. When this Chakra is blocked physical ailments can show themselves as headaches, anxiety and worry.

Vibrations of the Chakras

All the chakras have a different frequency at which they vibrate and have a different sound, color and symbol associated with each. Anytime a chakra is energized, clear and balanced, it would play its own sound harmoniously, sending out the right vibration for that specific chakra.

Several objects can affect vibrations, including gemstones, (which color vibrational energy), as well as mantras, chants, music, drums, and the sound of the voice.

All sounds and colors have their own vibrations, and making use of the chakras' colors and sounds will help them to become balanced and aligned. The chakras reflect the colors of the rainbow, beginning in order with the main chakra (black/red), then orange, yellow, green/pink, light blue, then indigo, and violet/white for the last chakra.

Every chakra has to be able to work on its own and at the right frequency. Each has to have some form of balance, must spin properly, and be energized and clear. Every time the chakras get to a particular stage of harmony, overall physical vibration is increased in the human body.

Imagine a scale from 1 to 10, with 10 as the highest point on the scale. As soon as each chakra gets to the same number, the whole spiritual, mental, emotional, and physical body rises to that new state of vibration equal to the chakras. The more work is done on chakra energy, the higher the entire body will move up on the scale, with the highest point being the point of enlightenment while the individual is still physically in a human body.

Blocked and Unbalanced Chakras Lead To Illness

As soon as the chakras stop spinning or vibrating properly, you are no longer able to bring your mental, emotional or physical body to the next spiritual level. As soon as we are born, we carry the imbalance or balance from former lives along with our spirit.

Every chakra has an effect on different areas of the body and many illnesses result from an unhealthy chakra.

We are provided with hints and perceptions all the time about what should be done to attain balance, and how we should conduct our lives. But we tend to ignore these hunches from our higher selves and from Spirit.

We become caught up in the physicality and reality of life and pay attention to our inner selves instead. The chakras become unbalanced, and the imbalance is manifested by affecting a physical part of the body.

When chakra blocks exist, your spiritual connection, life force and Chi tend to slow down. You might become listless, have difficulty thinking clearly, be tired, feel as if something is missing, or feel disconnected and even depressed. You may even become angry for no reason, have a negative perception of life, or feel sad for no apparent reason. You may feel a lack self-worth, a lack of trust in yourself, and be generally afraid. All of the above indicate problems that need to be resolved through the chakras.

Balanced Chakras Lead to Health and Happiness

ULEK (universal love, energy and knowledge) flows throughout the chakras. It is essential that you attempt to keep the right flow of energy going through each chakra. (When you have a chakra that is too open it can cause problems as well.) Balance in all and balance in each is what you are trying to maintain.

When the chakras are balanced and aligned, the energy will flow freely from the original base to the spiritual, providing that grounding necessary to achieve a higher level of spiritual communication. The aim is to have the same amounts of energy running through so that the flow of universal love, energy and knowledge is constant.

Using Chakras to Cure Yourself

Consider how you react when you get scared or become uncomfortable. Your stomach starts to churn. This is a reflection of an unsettled chakra. As soon as the fear fades, the stomach settles down and goes back to normal.

The whole body can react depending on the concerns and emotions that you bring with you. Issues in childhood and past lives can manifest as illnesses even though you may not be aware of them.

Not every physical ailment is the result of an imbalanced chakra - human beings do suffer from ailments.

On a spiritual level, we select the body that we occupy, or the body is selected by the Spirit for a specific reason that allows assimilation of knowledge to take place.

The work involving chakras is neither painless nor easy. Too often we think we have solved some issue on a mental level and emotional clutter can still be linked to the chakra. There is also a tendency to suppress things and this gets stored at a cellular level in the body. It will take a bit of work to clear those issues. Stones and crystals may help when working with the chakras.

Working with chakras involves transition. Transitions will be made from one level of physical vibration to the next; you may then go through a period of adjustment where you feel as if you are stuck in two places before settling into the new level.

As soon as the chakras are settled, there will be new issues to deal with. You may find that you are not able to deal with all of them. You may discover something blocking an issue or issues. As soon as you get rid of *that* block, some other issue will arise.

When something is completely resolved, you will feel it all over spiritually (feeling the change to love that is unconditional), mentally (gaining a higher level of understanding), emotionally (screaming or crying) and physically.

Take caution even when you feel an issue is resolved, it may return, or you may not have fully cleared all the spiritual concerns, reasons and emotions connected with this problem.

You may never really know if a chakra is clear, but you will know when something is released after it has been embraced.

As you move from one level to the next, you may need help facing new challenges as they manifest. Psychiatrists and psychologists assist us with our emotional and mental problems, which help keep the chakras in harmony. Spiritually, assistance is offered by rabbis, priests, preachers and energy healers.

Doctors help with the physical aspects. Each individual plays a role in healing the chakras. With a good team, you will be well on your way to improving your whole being.

The 7 Chakras all play important parts in our daily routines. From the way we think, to the way we love and treat others, every Chakra has a part to play. Understanding how these Chakras affect us and our energy levels is the first part of doing something to correct them. Knowing their purpose and how to deal with them can seriously improve our lives.

Chapter 4: Reiki And Spiritual Healing

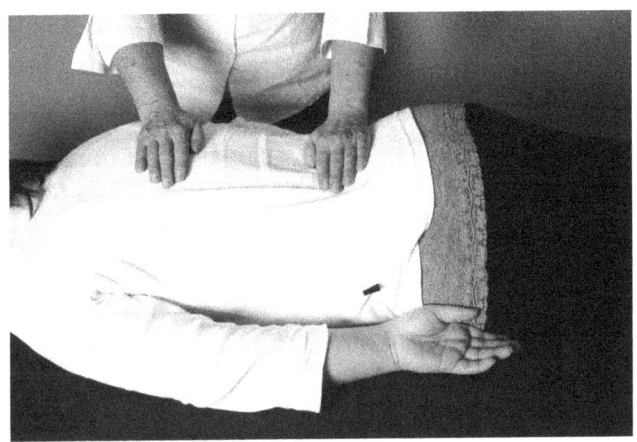

Relaxation and stress reduction are two of the best healing benefits of Reiki. It maintains and improves upon health by triggering the natural healing abilities of the body. This form of therapy is natural and apart from making the recipient healthy and well also helps to balance the life energies.

It is a non-invasive, easy system that works with the Receiver or Higher Self to promote well-being and health for the whole psychic, emotional and physical body. It happens to be a great way to promote and attain wholeness of Spirit, Body and Mind.

Reiki is a particular form of work with faint energy through which healing is carried out through the use of the hands of the Reiki practitioners to touch various areas of the body causing the flow of energy from an infinite source of power to the person being healed. It is a very gentle yet powerful energy which can be channeled with ease to others and yourself with intention alone.

This type of healing is a pure form of energy. When it is mixed with the honest desire of the Healee (person seeking healing) that has no problems getting cleansing done in their spiritual and emotional consciousness the healing will take effect.

Possible Health Benefits of Healing Treatments Using Reiki

Anytime there is a disruption on the life force energy or it is blocked or weakened, health or emotional problems will happen. This lack of balance can be caused by a number of situations that happen in life. These may be negative feelings and thoughts like an unhealthy expression of emotions, no love for others or for self, neglecting oneself, anxiety, doubt, worry and fear, injury, physical or emotional trauma.

Reiki is one of the best options to heal any spiritual, emotional, mental and physical issues as it gives wonderful results.

A Few of the Advantages of Reiki Healing:

Causes relaxation and helps the rid the body of tension and stress

Speeds up the ability of the body to heal naturally

Helps with sleep

Lowers blood pressure

Assists with chronic (headaches, eczema and asthma) and acute issues (injuries) as well as the elimination of addictions

Provides relief from pain

Regulates the flow of energy in the endocrine system and gets rid of blockages to energy allowing the body to get back in harmony and balance.

Help the body to get rid of toxins

Lowers a few of the side effects of medications and also assists the body to bounce back from drug therapy following chemotherapy and surgery.

Boosts the immune system

Slows down the process of aging and boosts vitality

Increases vibrational frequency

Aids in emotional clearing and spiritual growth

Anytime an individual is stress free and relaxed they can get back the natural healing ability.

Practicing full body Reiki for the long haul will get the body back in balance. It will free up the channels of energy and permit the body to naturally and effectively deal with depression and anxiety, the accumulation of toxins and stress.

When an individual is healthy, doing therapy on a regular basis will boost the built in defenses of the body. This will show itself as outward harmony and confidence when going about daily tasks. The individual will have an optimistic stance on life.

Reiki also tends to provide the individual with the energy needed to get over illnesses.

A healing session of Reiki can bring on an exceptionally relaxed state that can trigger a change in the consciousness of the client.

If utilized with other therapies that are natural (homeopathy, Bach flower remedies, aromatherapy, crystals meditation and so on...) Reiki will boost the effects they have.

It can be utilized as a complementary form of therapy as Reiki is really a form of care that goes well with something else. It improves the health care the individual receives from other health care practitioners or from the hospital.

This form of healing meshes Western and Eastern medicine and everyone can benefit from it. It is essential to the health of children, men and women (whether they are pregnant or not). It also works well for plants and animals (horses, cats and dogs).

This form of healing energy is a tool that can be utilized at any moment, any location and any location to relieve pain and get rid of stress on the spot as well as provide a quick boost of energy.

Reiki System - The Usui System

This natural form of healing has its origins in Tibet. The name Reiki is derived from the techniques that were re-instated by a Japanese Buddhist named Dr. Mikao Usui that lived in the early part of the twentieth century.

Universal mean "Re" and it is typically used to represent unseen spiritual quality of spirit which serves as a channel for life source energy "ki". Some refer to it as Love Energy, Prana, Qi, Chi, Buddha or God or something similar. It includes all the all-encompassing superior universal energy that all of the other lesser energies in the cosmos get their power.

All things in the cosmos are made up from aspects of energy which make up the all knowledgeable, omniscient draft for creation. This life force appears in various expressions of energy and Reiki stemmed from one of these.

This natural healing Usui system also teaches us the secret of getting happiness in one's life that can be achieved by utilizing one of the Three Degrees of Attunements and Five Reiki Ideals. The latter helps us to learn that making self-improvements is vital to healing from Reiki.

How the Healing Energy of Reiki Works?

The body is not just a set of parts that function. As everything emits a frequency, the organs found in the body possess their own field of energy which changes all the time. All the symptoms of disease are found in this system of energy. If the life force is blocked or low there is an increased likelihood that sickness will manifest. If it is flowing freely and high we can maintain our well-being and health.

The healing energy of Reiki gives us the method to put the Chakras and Auras in balance (energy centers and human energy fields respectively) which provides the conditions required for the body that is in the process of healing to function.

The practitioners of Reiki will help the client to heal themselves physically, emotionally, mentally and spiritually by laying on the hands. Through the use of old healing symbols the practitioners are able to channel the life force energy of the cosmos and allowing it to go where it is required to align the energy centers.

This individual also has to be an unblocked vessel through which the energy of healing flows. The practitioners will have a vital role in part of the process of healing, but in the long run it is up to the persons seeking healing to cause balance and harmony in their lives.

Meet the Author

Author and healer Stacy Milescu leads her life toward peace and wellness. She has years of experience in the areas of spiritual healing, holistic health, yoga, and meditation. Through these disciplines, she is able to help people work through seasons of stress, grief, or injury, and also to find clarity and drive during more comfortable times.

Stacy first encountered yoga and meditation in 2004. She found herself nearly overwhelmed by anxiety while her husband was fighting cancer, and a friend suggested yoga as an option for centering herself. She quickly became interested in meditation and holistic health as well. With the help of a spiritual advisor and a fantastic yoga instruction, she regained her breath and survived those scary years. Now she and her husband—cancer free for almost 8 years now—do yoga together a couple times a week!

When she is not pursuing wellness, Stacy is generally enjoying time with her fantastic husband Gabe and their two boys Jake and Evan. As a family, they enjoy playing card games. She tends to lose at Euchre, but wins at Poker. She likes to think her penchant for serenity helps her poker face.

MORE BOOKS BY STACY MILESCU

Yoga For Beginners: A Complete Guide on Yoga for Beginners

www.ingramcontent.com/pod-product-compliance
Ingram Content Group UK Ltd.
Pitfield, Milton Keynes, MK11 3LW, UK
UKHW022119230426